I0162974

What the Rain Said Last Night

—*Travels After Loss*—

CHLOE VINER

FUTURECYCLE PRESS

www.futurecycle.org

Copyright © 2015 Chloe Viner
All Rights Reserved

Published by FutureCycle Press
Lexington, Kentucky, USA

ISBN 978-1-938853-85-2

To my husband, Shane Collins,
who taught me how to treat writing as a discipline.
Without his thoughtful feedback and encouragement,
this book would not have been possible.

Contents

—Part 1, Out West—

Fused

—*Manhattan, New York*—

There was a mangled mesh
of wires in a protruding clump
in the sole of my right foot.
Every step sent
electric currents through my veins
large buildings collapsing
behind me as I slowly progressed
crumbling into toxic masses of black
air and concrete.
I sat on a pile of rubble
tried to slice the metal from my flesh
but it was so entwined
there was no part where that steel trap ended
and I began.

I wandered past an Italian restaurant
steaming plates of alfredo
delicately arranged basil leafs
following the smell of tomatoes and garlic.
Heads raised
people covered their mouths
with their manicured palms
wondering where this molten mess of wires
had come from.

Bedraggled

—Philadelphia, Pennsylvania—

There is something inherently sad
about a wet dog.
People don't react the same way
to a man in the alley
or the businessman in the
killer black suit
smoking away his infidelities
trying to hide his weakness for stewardesses and
boredom with stock exchanges

thinking he can pass them off
as spare change
and then understand his destiny.
But even the chai latte is silent when he probes it

like the faded edges of a receipt
soggy and forgotten
like a dog
a man
the shell of a man.
They all look the same when the rain
comes
and leaves them
standing on street corners
waiting for the light to change.

Vacancy

—Baltimore, Maryland—

Even in the sand she leaves no footprints.
The second her foot makes a vacancy
it is filled by rushing stone particles.
She has no shadow
nothing to mark where she has been
the first piece of paper in a notebook
torn and tossed to accommodate for error.

There is a jar by her front door and
every day she empties her expectations into it
afternoon callouses and tangerine-colored eyeglasses.
She hopes to retrieve them the next day
but every morning when she wakes the jar is empty.

An old pencil from middle school
the eraser more likely to leave sunset-colored
rubber streaks across the page then to undo what has been written
a tire rotation that merely reorients the same thread-bald rubber
a soda that tastes sickeningly sweet and the same at every
fast food restaurant
potholes, fevers, children waiting at bus stops
knowing that the bus will take them to the same place every day.

There is nothing at her bottom
nothing at the bottom of the bottle or the pipe or the
art she bares.

A sea critter desperately seeking a new shell
finding only sea glass and old newspapers
nothing to mold a home out of
like the Old Man and the Sea
desperately struggling to bring a worthy catch to shore
but lucky to escape with his life.

Frail, old, tired, bloodied palms
only a skeleton left.

Red Dress

—Washington, DC—

Washing machines break
trees fall
cars accumulate
animals scavenge—
somewhere between wheels of poison
and blooming body parts
is a small red dress
that belonged to a girl
who jumped rope and disappeared
into the sidewalk
swallowed by cement
leaving her tears in puddles
and her red dress blowing in the
wind.

Zachary

—Blacksburg, Virginia—

On Saturdays we would jump on the old trampoline
in the backyard between big oak trees
shading us just enough to keep the sun at bay
like waves that never reach the towel at the beach.
Light has no limits—
any color can be seen through a glass prism.

You were always laughing.
Not always like "it always rains in Seattle"
always like the husband loves his wife—
it touches everything.
That's the way your laughter spread
its sparkling wisps across the yard
gentleness easing out of you the way
a baby bear comes out after a long winter
eager and ready to try everything.

Mardi Gras parades—
all that noise and color still didn't
compare to you.
I hear your laughter more than I see your face.
You are something the world cannot replace.

Feathers

—Myrtle Beach, South Carolina—

Dreams fall like feathers
litter the shore
among old soda bottles and plastic shopping bags
waiting for the day that they are swept
into the ocean
where a fisherman may accidentally reel one in
bring its brilliance into his home.

In a town where children are born of falling feathers
men roam the shores in desperation
seeking lost dreams
but finding only faded
sea glass.

Carriage Rides

—Orleans Parish, Louisiana—

A horse hoof
hits concrete
like an alcoholic's glass
reverberating on the bar
alerting the world to its
misfortune.

Lovers fall into one another's arms
in overly priced suits
forgetting that horses and men
once found solace
in grass and planes.

This foreign delight
the taste of paprika
making his senses fold
like the sheets on a bed
tightly tucked in
at every corner.

Maybe some Monday morning
we can catch a ride and
end up in the middle of the desert
far away from this place.

Strawberries and Nostalgia

—New Orleans Zoo, Louisiana—

Flamingos are pink because they consume
eleven shrimp a day.
You can trace the origins of anyone's
demeanor back to consumption.

I feel colors
taste shapes
and dance in the footprints of orange peels
tossing the pits aside
blooming with strawberries and nostalgia
forgoing the familiar
until people's jaws drop
and they wonder
what I
eat.

Disposal

—Lower Ninth Ward New Orleans, Louisiana—

There is a thin line
that divides the highway from
the sickly swerving side
of town.

The black and white
crumpled papers
soda cans
layers of bruises
cigarettes on lazy armchairs
leaving their mark
in the fabric
like a soiled diaper
forgotten in the heat of the moment.

Mice and vermin
eat the wallpaper
streaks of smoke
dye the sheets
and the mattress smells
of death.

The sound of the train
rumbles everything like a salt shaker
turned upside down
parts flying out the window
to season the sidewalk
with the pigment of putrefaction.

Small Town

—Jackson, Mississippi—

She flips flapjacks
takes orders
wears a faded yellow apron
dons jaded like it is her work ethic
serves up mud pies of frustration
services truckers like a mechanic
swapping oil for coffee—

a cheerleader
twenty years later
saggy and frayed
pom-poms in the gutter with the rest of the
casualties.

She taps her pencil on the counter and
remembers something
about the mythological phoenix
one wing compassion
the other wisdom.
Here birds are found in alleys
in parking lots
and in halfway houses.

She shakes her head and tosses aside the pencil
punches in her hours
sweeps up bird carcasses and twisted radios
goes home.
Tomorrow the holy mess
is made again.

Depression

—Chicago, Illinois—

He didn't see the humor in funerals but
decided not to tell her
as they piled into his black Chevy
and rolled away from the end of his life.

The lines on the highway blurred
dividing him from the rest of the world
emphasizing those differences which had always been there
with a cruel and mocking finality.

The world went left as he turned right.
He fell through the old leather seat cushions
and sank into the cement
lost between car seats and an old shiny nickel.

Smashing Plate Room

—Saint Paul, Minnesota—

The sound of breaking glass makes for startling music
shards and slivers slicing through sound waves
highs and lows highlighted by
blue rims on plate borders.
Circling the floor, a hawk eagerly eyes its prey.
Its prey is the sound of s*mashing.*
Breaking is so erotic
it's foreplay for your anger
clashing, smashing, thrashing, and crashing
fitting all that frustration in four corners.

A tambourine is simply more civil than I'm willing to be.
Won't you come smash plates with me?

Circles

—Jamestown, North Dakota —

Cigarette burns line her wrist like
polka dots on a fall sweater
the little dots making up a snowman
(or a happier childhood).
Scars zigzag across her thighs
where a razor made its way on Saturday evenings while
the television blared loudly and the smell of
gin soaked through
the peeling paper walls
where she tried to find a line between emotions
and her insides
but was left holding only pale steel
while drops sprinkled the floor
and cigarette butts burned
so many circles.

Dark areas under her eyes
light cast by a flashlight in a closet
skittering sounds
too many circles.

Own Worst Enemy

—Billings, Montana—

Plaster on the wall
covers up the spot where we used to aim
our cigarette smoke
as we plucked feathers from the couch cushions
listened to football
on the TV we got at the dump
rescued from life in a landfill
like us.

Playing tic-tac-toe
on an old phone book
while a mouse eases its way toward the coffee table.

I pick up the old rusty trophy on the mantel
you pick up your sneakers from the carpet
toss them into the tub
so the mud won't get everywhere
but both of us know
dirt clings to this apartment.

We paste photos on the walls
pretend they are windows into
our future.
Nothing comes to change us
so we stay and crumble
with the walls.

Artist's Peak

— Yellowstone Park, Wyoming —

Sewing a waterfall
stitches fall to the sides
splashes of cloth
soaking into the seams.

Ripples growing into small mountains
hug the water like a
small child stretching her arms
around her grown father
unable
to touch fingers
unable to mend loose stitches
just a small splash

prickly bushes
like finger tips
tracing their way along the brim
feeling for subtle trends
in the fabric
teasing the water's edge
and merging.

Ticktock is lost here
nothing so cloying
nothing so confining
just the colors of the thread
and the grey wolves' howls
as they feed on deer
and taste the sweetness of red
like a child licking ice cream from her fingers.

Dragonfly

—Jackson, Wyoming—

I play with fire
because the blisters on my fingertips
remind me
of the heat of your lips.

I turn the steering wheel down
the highway
as we slide in close
laugh at fireworks
sleep in the tree's hollow trunk
pack nothing
leave the setting sun
to say our goodbyes.

Drifting down railroad tracks
the noise comforts us
as our mothers' rocking once did
steam blows from the engine
as we remember
what the rain said last night.

Sensitivity

—Logan, Utah—

I don't watch the news anymore.
I worry one more pulse will send
a shard to an artery.

I watch a sunset the way
an inmate
on death row tastes his last meal
feeling every hue
a starving man finding flavor.

I smell fragrances like a bride
choosing floral arrangements
the way an old joint feels rain
coming.

I love the way a mother
first holds her infant and won't let go
I don't want the world to scrub you clean
and bring you back
smelling of powder and linen.

Withdraw

—Denver, Colorado—

Elephants are known to return to
cemeteries and cry.
Human beings like to think they hold a monopoly
on that kind of suffering.

If you withdrew into caves
balanced yourself between stalactites and stalagmites
you could fill the gap between the two.

The taste of iron is found in stale water and blood
reminding us that we too can grow old and musty
fall to the wayside and taste like
burnt amber.

Inside caves and by tombstones
we leave behind weeping elephants
bask in empty hugs and cursory waves
think a ticket is worth a skipped heartbeat
when not even
graveyards are.

Siren

—Albuquerque, New Mexico—

His discomfort is a drop of ink in a bowl of water
permeating every cell.
Meandering through the marketplace
he pauses to choose between an iris and a purple bracelet.

He imagines the iris on her windowsill
its white petals curling inward
competing with her stoic beauty.
The purple bracelet on her thin wrist
slowing her down like a handcuff
shattering to the ground leaving
purple fragments of his thoughtfulness.

He leaves the marketplace empty-handed
gets home, curls into bed and holds her and
everything he has ever given her smashes, breaks, dies, and pales.
He clings to her knowing that he will never be able to contain her
and in the morning she is gone.

A small pale blue lily rests on the bed where she slept.
He carries its petals in his pocket and they whisper to him
that he will not be alone forever.

First Time

—Border between Arizona and Mexico—

Basements of pianos
keys everywhere
in your underwear
and in your hair.
When you walk down the street
it sounds like a five-year-old
has just placed his hands
on a musical instrument for the first time.

Paper Thin

—Kingman, Arizona—

She is a paper puppet
casting weaving shadows
too thin to maintain the movement.
Edges crumple and tear
twirling into backstage corners
facing off with angry mice
caught up in a tangle of webs
spiraling into the depths of the basement.
Nothing here.
Above the show is in climax—
laughter swells, hands clap, comical one-liners are yelled—
the world does not know that downstairs
the delicate puppet
is dying.

Weeping into sawdust
her paper hands try to absorb her ink tears
words streaming down her face
letters collecting in her tunic
soggy leaflets crumpling into puddles.

By the time the curtain is drawn
she is no more.
Only the janitor notices her small ragged heap after hours.
He takes her broken body home and places it in his windowsill
so she can see the sunrise.

One More Hand

—Las Vegas, Nevada—

"Play your cards right"
he said and winked
but he was no King of Hearts.
He wasn't even a Jack of Clubs
just a homely Seven of Spades
faded and folded in at the edges.

A long time ago
when he was glossy
she might have played one hand with him
just to see if he could fall into the right spot
and make something of himself.

She thought briefly about playing a new game—
craps or maybe even some slots—
but she knew cards
and found comfort in their numbers.
Like a sailor putting his feet on solid ground
she dealt the cards
and tried not to smile
at her royal straight flush.

If only men were such.

Yard Sales

—Sacramento, California—

She tossed out the bag of her twenties
and sold her thirties for $4.50
and sat on her forties
while contemplating the piano and
the for-sale sign on the lawn.

Koalas

—San Francisco Zoo, California—

Koala bears eat 67 pounds of bamboo a day.
Americans check 67 emails a day.
They are both tired and hungry.

Raindrop Envy

—Portland, Oregon—

I wish I were a raindrop
plip plop.
I'd shimmy down windowsills
silky-smooth and sensual.
I'd nourish the earth and smell its musty aftershave.
I'd burrow into the crevices and come out in twinkles.
Rinse and repeat.

I'd rather *plip plop* on the pavement
than return to a place that can never be home
to nurture the unnurturable
and mend the unfixable
while water runs in the tub
and I drown in the living room.

Stone Warm

—Rockaway Beach, Washington—

The stone is an old man hunched over a wicker table
slowly stitching the seam of a sea-worn tarp.
It is a frail woman placing her clip-on earrings by the windowsill
where light reflects the time that has passed in jagged
patterns across the wall.
It is a young child dropping pebbles down a well
waiting for the resounding *ping* of contact
to reassure him that nothing is
endless.

Taste Me!

—Seattle, Washington—

I leave my words like the baker leaves fresh dough to rise
hoping in time the yeast will give it a full body.
Instead my words hang, fall to the ground
are swept away at the end of the day.
My offerings in the trash have no impact
on coffee grounds and crumpled paper.

I come to the café every morning
and order a large chai latte.
I am there to see the baker
who wipes flour on his old apron
brushes my words aside, doesn't give them
the tenderness he kneads pastry dough with.
I hunger for the day he will add each word I say
to the muffin batter
so the kid in the corner on his Mac might taste
my passion mingling with the blueberry notes.

—Part 2, Abroad—

Bayonet

—Athens, Greece—

If you had a bayonet
could you wield it in an efficient capacity?
Sluicing through the air and creating wind power?
Finding in it salvation?

Most men cannot.

They are tasked with the impenetrable duty
of watching time tick by as they do nothing.
The weight of that *nothing* can be massive.
More draining than Atlas's duty—
continents digging into shoulder blades
oceans dripping salty sweat down his forearms.
Would you drop the whole writhing mess into the depths of space?
Or sacrifice eternity to hold onto
squabbling men and
forgotten arts?

She Was an Hourglass

—Ho Chi Minh, Vietnam—

She was an hourglass—
no, a sieve—
because what filtered through disappeared
leaving her hollowed out.
She flitted by in orange silk
pausing to push butterflies from their
sentry posts on rosebuds.

They bubble-wrapped her insides.
When we opened them, we found
stale air and broken glass
drops of perspiration, pages of old novels
shells, crusts, containers,
a picked-over tombstone
emptiness between cliffs
space between waves
room between grains of sand
the place between hands
on a steering wheel.

Identity Theft

—London, England—

He pickpocketed
liked to get close to people—
to enter their inner sanctum
without their knowledge
was a sensual experience.

Holding their wallets was holding their hearts
trying out their names on his tongue
to see if they tasted like their breath did when
he was inches away.

He liked to become them
swallowing up their suits
pursuing their women
using their toothbrushes—
the more intimate, the more
erotic.

Wax

—Florence, Italy—

She liked riding on his shoulders
could reach the lower leaves of trees
before they turned colors completely.

She would take leaves home
iron them between two pieces of wax paper.
They would stay the same there
forever sealed in that moment and wax.
She wondered if that could happen to her
frozen on her father's shoulders
while someone mounted them on a wall
or placed them on a coffee table.

That way she would not be raked up and piled
hauled to the curb in oversized black and green trash bags.

Unsettled

—Budapest, Hungary—

A pot of boiling water overflowing.
Skidding on the ice as you
press the breaks in the snow.
A plane hitting a pocket of turbulence.
Hair that stands on end as
the dentist files down teeth.
Waking up quickly
after falling into yourself
biting your nails to the quick.
Standing from a hot tub
the world filled with black splotches.
Smelling burnt stove cleaner
and tasting city rain.
That moment when for no reason
you are unsettled again.

June

—Aguadilla, Puerto Rico—

I was a drenched cat crying at the door
hoping you would let me in.
Like plates stacked in the kitchen cupboard
pulled out for special occasions
I would keep my awe for you
safely tucked away
so I could surprise you with
it on special
occasions.

Kissing on a sweaty June day
holding each other like a drunk man
grasps to a railing
trying to hide how the world spins around him.

You're a bathtub overflowing
soaking the floor
and I'm left leaving soapy footprints of
how much I love you
everywhere I
step.

Acknowledgments

Grateful acknowledgment is made to the following publications in which these poems first appeared.

Eskimo Pie: "Bedraggled"
Grey Wolf Publishing: "Bayonet"
Mad Swirl Poetry Forum: "Yard Sales"
Poetry Quarterly: "Artist's Peak," "Disposal," "Fused"
Poetry Super Highway: "Own Worst Enemy"

Cover artwork, "Rain," by Griszka Niewiadomski; author photo by Shane Collins; cover and interior book design by Diane Kistner; Caudex text and titling

About FutureCycle Press

FutureCycle Press is dedicated to publishing lasting English-language poetry books, chapbooks, and anthologies in both print-on-demand and ebook formats. Founded in 2007 by long-time independent editor/publishers and partners Diane Kistner and Robert S. King, the press incorporated as a nonprofit in 2012. A number of our editors are distinguished poets and writers in their own right, and we have been actively involved in the small press movement going back to the early seventies.

The FutureCycle Poetry Book Prize and honorarium is awarded annually for the best full-length volume of poetry we publish in a calendar year. Introduced in 2013, our Good Works projects are anthologies devoted to issues of universal significance, with all proceeds donated to a related worthy cause. Our Selected Poems series highlights contemporary poets with a substantial body of work to their credit; with this series we strive to resurrect work that has had limited distribution and is now out of print.

We are dedicated to giving all of the authors we publish the care their work deserves, making our catalog of titles the most diverse and distinguished it can be, and paying forward any earnings to fund more great books.

We've learned a few things about independent publishing over the years. We've also evolved a unique, resilient publishing model that allows us to focus mainly on vetting and preserving for posterity the most books of exceptional quality without becoming overwhelmed with bookkeeping and mailing, fundraising activities, or taxing editorial and production "bubbles." To find out more about what we are doing, come see us at www.futurecycle.org.

www.ingramcontent.com/pod-product-compliance
Lightning Source LLC
Chambersburg PA
CBHW060043050426
42448CB00012B/3116